THE ESSENT
Dining Etiquette

A Guide to Understanding and Mastering Dining Rules

TAMLYN FRANKLIN

The Essentials of Dining Etiquette
Copyright ©2016 Tamyln Franklin

ISBN-13: 978-1540592927
ISBN-10: 1540592928

All rights reserved. The Essentials of Dining Etiquette is a presentation of The Etiquette Consulting Group, LLC. No part of this publication may be reproduced, stored in a retrieval system, or transmitted in any form or by any means: electronic, mechanical, photo copying, recording or otherwise – without prior written permission from Tamlyn Franklin, President, Etiquette Consulting Group, LLC.

Table of Contents

Foreword vii

Table Manners: Seating 1

Table Manners: Eating 3

Place Setting 5

Place Setting – What is mine? 7

Place Setting – Which Fork Do I Use? 9

Napkin Etiquette 15

Correct Silverware Usage 19

Eating Meat 21

American Style 23

American Style – 25

Continental Style 27

Continental Style – 29

Utensils/Flatware 31

Table Manners Guidelines 35

Guidelines: How To Eat Difficult Foods 51

Manners Basics 57

Dress Appropriately 59

Posture. 61

Conversations at the Table 63

Dinner Table Etiquette 65

Acknowledgements

There are many who helped with this book.

- ❖ Thank you Almighty God for giving me the strength and courage to complete this project.

- ❖ Mom and Dad: Thank you for teaching me so much about life and helping to shape who I am.

- ❖ My sister: A big hug to Gwendolyn Jackson who is a constant source of encouragement and who is always willing to lend a hand, literally.

- ❖ Special thanks to my loving and selfless cousin, Sheli Harris, for your editing revisions and tireless efforts.

- ❖ My deepest thanks to my mother-in-law, Virginia L. Franklin whose helpful feedback and editing genius helped to make this book what it is.

- ❖ All of my children, especially Destiny and Cordell: my youngest two, who have more patience than they know. I love you dearly.

- ❖ Grandma Sis: You are the wisest and toughest person I know. I love you so much.

- ❖ Kimmoly Rice Ogletree: Thank you for your love, friendship, and support.

- ❖ Carolyn: Thank you for the book layout.

- ❖ Lynn, Tracey, and Censeria: Thank you for always being in my corner and saying something to keep me going.

- ❖ Finally and most importantly, much love to my husband and best friend, Troy. You understand me and support me, no matter what. Your love and support is the reason for many of my accomplishments. I value your input and cherish you endlessly.

Foreword

This workbook is intended for the person who seeks to understand and master the rules of dining. The person could be a blooming teen, a young adult or a mature adult—someone entering or exiting school, college, or the work force. This workbook is a reference for preparing for a date, a prom, a cotillion, an engagement, a wedding, a ball, or some other important social or business function that involves dining. It's also for the person who just wants to hone additional skills for self improvement.

The objective of this workbook is to provide guidance that will help one master dining rules. In this workbook you will find instructions and explanations of the dining experience from start to finish—from taking your seat to exiting the table at the conclusion of a meal—and yes, everything in between. This book includes the essentials of dining etiquette. You will also find some helpful tips on time management, how to use specific utensils, how to eat difficult foods, and some basic dining guidelines. Following the guidelines and instructions given herein will ensure the following benefits:

- ❖ Provide clarity in the use of dining flatware, dishes, and glassware.

- ❖ Give you the confidence you need to navigate through any dining occasion. People gravitate toward those who project self-confidence.

- ❖ Enhance your professional image. A polished professional image will give you a competitive advantage and help you stand out from the crowd.

- ❖ Help you avoid common dining mistakes that can ruin relationships.

- ❖ Improve personal and business relationships.

- ❖ Can ultimately impact the number of professional opportunities that you are afforded.

- ❖ Could help you secure a job offer or promotion.

- ❖ Promote lifelong success and professional development.

As you look through the pages of this workbook, be sure to highlight appropriate sections for later reference. Rest assured, there is enough information between these pages to allow you to master the rules of banqueting and even become an aficionado of dining etiquette. Now let's learn the rules of dining.

Table Manners: Seating

Seating Yourself

- Lefties (at left end or head of table)

- Enter your seat from the right and exit from the left

- Take your seat
  - Pull the chair out.
  - Stand to the right of the chair.
  - Leading with your left side, step in front of the chair.
  - Back up until your legs touch the chair.
  - Lower yourself halfway.
  - Grasp the sides of the chair with both hands and pull the chair under you as you take your seat.

When Men Assist Women

- A gentleman seats a lady to the right (even if she did not accompany him).
  - Stand directly behind her chair with both hands grasping the chair back.
  - Gently pull out the chair.
  - When she is half-seated, gently push the chair under her. Ladies should assist by placing both hands on the sides of the chair as they are seated.

- Before sitting for a formal meal, gentlemen stand behind ladies' chairs until they are seated.

- Men's and unisex hats should never be worn at the table.

Table Manners: Eating

When to Start Eating?

      ഔ Wait for the host or hostess to begin eating before you do. This should be done for every course.

If there is no host…

      ഔ If there are **8** or less people at the table, wait until everyone has been served before you begin.

      ഔ If there is a **buffet,** wait until 3 other people have joined you before you begin.

      ഔ Never be the first to begin eating.

      ഔ Do not eat alone.

      ഔ Pace yourself with other diners so you are not the first or last to finish eating.

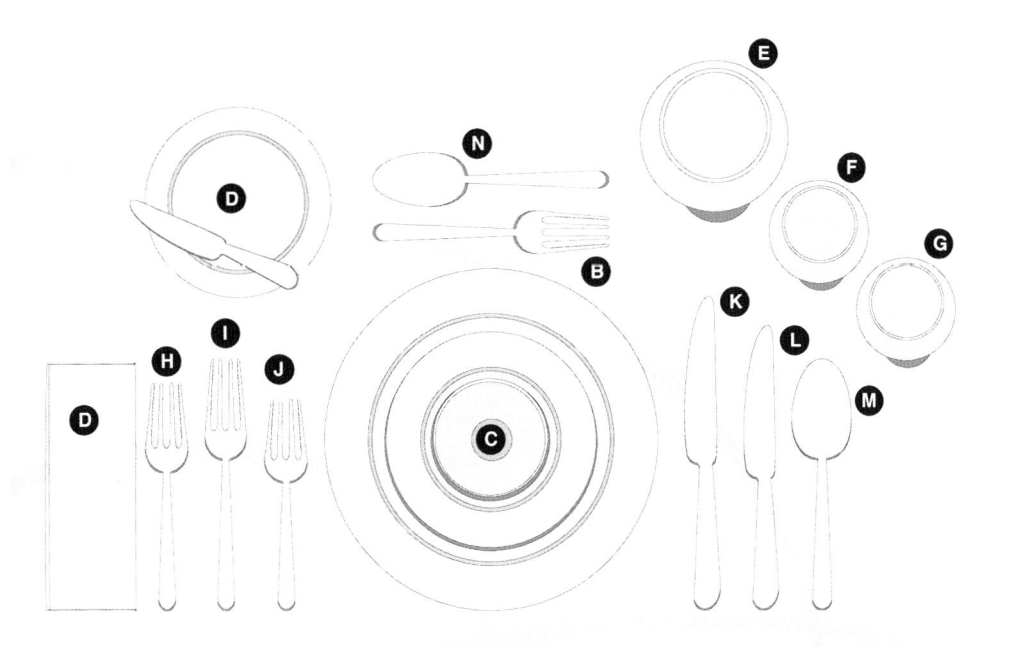

Place Setting

A – napkin

B – dinner plate

C – soup bowl

D – bread plate

E – water glass

F – white wine

G – red wine

H – fish fork

I – dinner fork

J – salad fork

K – dinner knife

L - fish knife

M – soup spoon

N – dessert spoon and cake fork

What is mine?   Bread   Main Course   Water
                          B- M- W

Place Setting –
What is mine?

The Place Setting

At a pre-set table where the place settings are very close, it can be difficult to tell which glass, napkin or coffee cup is yours. If the table is round, this can be more confusing. What are all these plates, glasses, and utensils? Which ones are to be used and when? Solve the problem by looking at the place setting in front of you. Your meal plate (main course) is always in the center. Your beverages (water, coffee, iced tea, etc.) are always located on your right. Solids, such as a bread plate or salad plate, are always on the left.

Reading the Table Setting

Business functions that involve formal or informal dining are intended to build business relationships. Inappropriate behavior, subpar manners and misuse of dinnerware can weaken or damage business relationships. It is a good idea to familiarize oneself with every utensil, glass, and plate that can be used and master how to use them. Albeit some dining rules overlap, there are different dining rules when attending different functions: an informal lunch, a formal business dinner, a dinner banquet or a five-course business function. Mastering the rules for each type of dining engagement will give you the confidence you need to focus on business.

Work from the Outside In- Always start with the utensil of each type that is farthest from the plate.

Formal Dinner

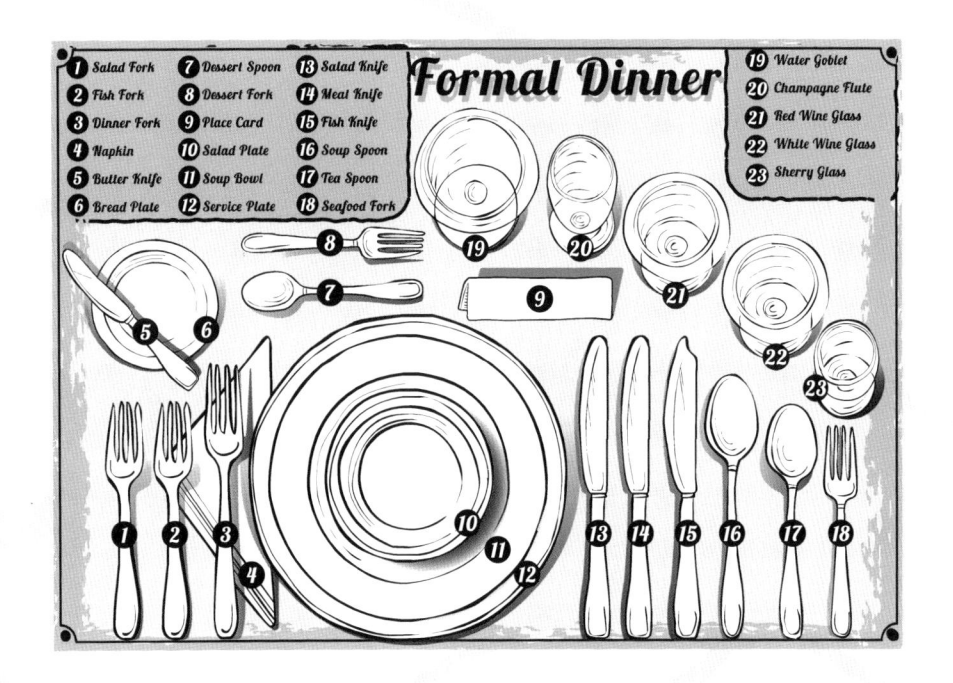

1. Salad Fork
2. Fish Fork
3. Dinner Fork
4. Napkin
5. Butter Knife
6. Bread Plate
7. Dessert Spoon
8. Dessert Fork
9. Place Card
10. Salad Plate
11. Soup Bowl
12. Service Plate
13. Salad Knife
14. Meat Knife
15. Fish Knife
16. Soup Spoon
17. Tea Spoon
18. Seafood Fork
19. Water Goblet
20. Champagne Flute
21. Red Wine Glass
22. White Wine Glass
23. Sherry Glass

Place Setting ~ Which Fork Do I Use?

Seafood Fork Etiquette

The seafood fork, the smallest of all forks, is used to remove the flesh from and to eat seafood (mussels, clams, lobster, crab, shrimp, and oysters)

Soup Spoon Etiquette

The soup spoon is made with a large or rounded bowl to accommodate the consistency of soup. Pickup the spoon with your dominant hand. Resting your thumb against the top of the spoon handle, hold the handle against the top of the middle finger and near the base of the index finger. Tilt the spoon away from you to fill the spoon, no more than two-thirds full to avoid spills. Soup is sipped from the side of the spoon (not the front).

Salad Fork and Salad Knife Etiquette

The placement of the salad fork and salad knife determines when the salad course will be served, whether before the main course or after the main course. According to this setting, the salad would be served after the main course.

Fish Knife and Fork Etiquette

The **fish knife** is used to break the fish apart or separate the soft flesh of the fish from the body rather than to cut a bite. The handle of the fish knife is held in the right hand, between the thumb, the middle and the index fingers, a position different than the way a dinner knife is held. The tip of the blade is used to fillet fish, lift the skeleton from the body, remove small bones and push it onto the fork. The **fish fork** is held in the left hand and used in the traditional way. If the fish is soft and boneless, you need use only the fork. Hold the fork in your right hand, tines up.

Dessert Fork and Dessert Spoon Etiquette

The dessert fork and dessert spoon are placed horizontally above the dinner plate (spoon handle facing to the right and the fork handle facing to the left). When dessert is served with both fork and spoon, the fork is used to push the dessert and the spoon is used for eating. The **dessert fork** is held in the left hand, tines downward. The **dessert spoon** is held in the right hand to take a bite to the mouth. Cake and pie require only a fork. Ice cream and pudding require only a spoon.

Dinner Knife and Dinner Fork Etiquette

The **dinner knife** may be used to spread butter if a butter knife is not provides and if it has not been used. At an informal meal, the dinner knife may be used for all courses. The dinner fork, the largest of all forks, is used for the main course.

Salad Fork and Salad Knife Etiquette

The placement of the salad fork and salad knife determines when the salad course will be served, whether before the main course or after the main course. According to this setting, the salad would be served after the main course.

Butter Knife Etiquette

The butter knife is located near (lying diagonally across the top of) the butter plate. Use the butter knife to transfer butter to your bread plate. Do not use the knife with the butter dish to butter your bread. If a butter knife is not provided, use your dinner knife to transfer butter to your bread plate.

Teaspoon Etiquette

While drinking coffee, avoid stirring coffee too much to prevent spills. Do not leave the spoon in the coffee cup. Place the soiled spoon on your saucer (not on the table). Proper table manners require that soiled utensils not be laid on the table after they are used. There is one exception to this rule. While drinking an iced beverage, hold the teaspoon in the glass against the rim with your index finger. The teaspoon remains in the glass until the glass is cleared from the table.

Napkin Etiquette

What you do with your napkin sends messages to others about your manners. What you do with your napkin also sends messages to the server about whether you are leaving the table for good or if you are coming back. Correct use of the napkin shows good manners and attention to details.

The meal begins when your host unfolds his or her napkin. Look for hints from the host and follow his/her lead.

In a banquet setting or at a restaurant, place your napkin in your lap as soon as you are seated. At more upscale restaurants, the server often will place your napkin on your lap for you, and when you leave the table temporarily, a member of the wait staff will bring you a fresh napkin and place it to the left of your plate.

Fold your napkin in half with the fold toward your waist, next to your body. The napkin remains on your lap throughout the entire meal.

Gently dab your napkin around your mouth to remove any liquid or food.

Instead of using all of your napkin, try to keep it clean and use an area around the same spot.

Don't clean up spills with your own napkin and don't touch items that have dropped on the floor.

Napkin placement - Not finished   Napkin placement - Finished

What do I do with my Napkin if I Need to Briefly Leave the Table?

If you need to leave the table during a meal, place the napkin on your chair, not on the table. Well-trained wait-staff know that when your napkin is on the chair, and not on the table, it means that you are coming back to the table.

What do I do with my Napkin when I am Finish with my Meal?

Place the napkin to the left of the plate. Wait for the hostess to do so first. If the plate has already been removed, put the napkin in the plate's place.

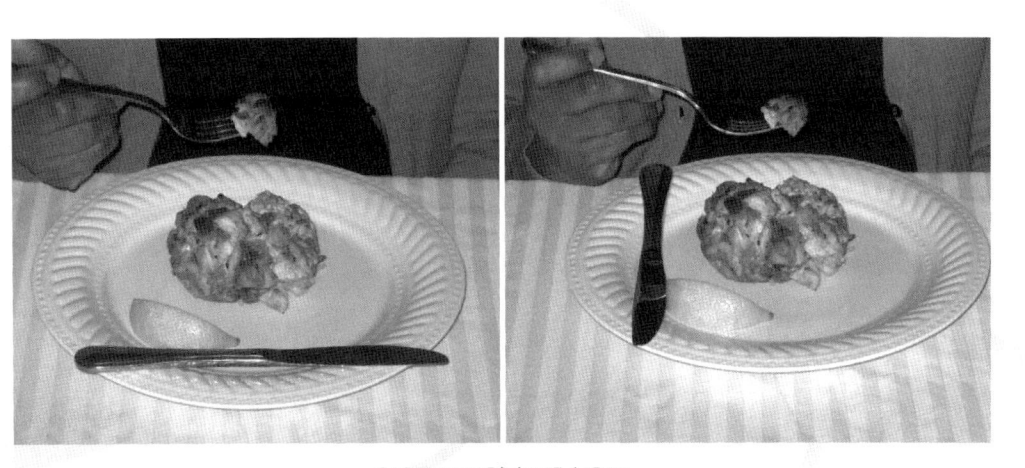

CORRECT USAGE:

Fork in right hand with the blade of knife facing you or facing your plate

Correct Silverware Usage

Hold the fork between your index finger and thumb, resting the fork on your middle finger about midway up the fork handle.

Clenched fists – INCORRECT   CORRECT

Eating Meat

Try to "cut" your meat, not "saw" it Hold the fork as though you were holding a pencil.

To cut meat, hold the fork in your left hand and the knife in right hand. Then switch the fork to your right hand to eat.

Cutting meat into small pieces - INCORRECT

**Don't cut up your meat
(fish, fowl, lamb, beef, etc.)
all at once.**

**Cut your meat and
eat one bite at a time.**

Eating American Style - CORRECT   Using a knife and fork - CORRECT

American Style
Using a knife and fork

In American Style, begin with the knife in your right hand and fork in your left hand. Cut your meat and then switch your fork to your right hand, from the left, put your knife down on the plate, spear a piece of meat, and then eat it.

American style - I'm not finished   American style - I'm finished

American Style –
What do I do with
my knife and fork during and after my meal?

When you have paused in eating but have not finished, leave your fork and knife in the position shown above on the left. Place your knife on the plate, diagonally on the upper right corner between cuttings (with the blade of your knife facing you).

When you leave your fork and knife on the side of the plate (4:20 on a clock face) in the position shown above on the right (the fork tines may face up or down), it signals to the waiter that you are through eating and that your plate may be removed.

Using a knife and fork - CORRECTLY

Continental Style
Using a knife and fork

In Continental or European Style, when you prepare to cut food, begin by placing the knife in your right hand and the fork in your left hand. To cut bite-size pieces of food, hold the food with the fork and cut with the knife. Then spear the food with the fork—which is still in your left hand—and put it in your mouth. Eat your food with the fork still in your left hand. The difference between American style and Continental style is that your fork stays in your left hand with the tines pointed down (do not switch hands).

Both utensils are kept in your hands with the fork tines pointed down throughout the entire eating process. If you take a drink, you do not only put your knife down, but you put both utensils down into the resting position: by crossing the fork over the knife as shown in the diagram on the next page (Continental style- I'm not finished).

Continental style - I'm finished    Continental style - I'm not finished

Continental Style -
What do I do with
My knife and fork during and after my meal?

When resting between bites (not finished), the knife and fork are crossed on the plate with the fork over the knife with the tines pointed down in an inverted V. The wait-staff is trained to not remove your plate with the knife and fork crossed because it indicates that you are not finished with your meal.

When you have completed your meal, the utensils are placed together (same as American style) on the plate, in the 4:20 clock face position, with the fork tines down.

Blade of knife facing out - INCORRECT

Utensil touching the table - INCORRECT

Utensils / Flatware

- Once a utensil is used, it should not touch the table (as shown above).

- The blade of your knife should be facing you or toward your plate; it should not be facing out, away from your plate (as shown above).

- Do not lift your flatware toward your face and inspect it; this is considered rude. If you notice that your flatware is soiled, quietly notify the wait staff; they will bring you new flatware.

- Use each utensil for its given purpose - That means that a salad fork should be used for your salad, and the soup spoon should be used for soup.

- Dirty flatware - If you drop flatware on the floor, it is dirty. DO NOT pick it up and DO NOT return it to the table. Notify the wait staff and they will retrieve it and provide you with a clean utensil.

- Save your fork only when asked by the hostess or wait staff. If additional utensils are required, they will be brought to you.

- Eating gracefully – Make every effort to hold utensils with the minimum amount of force required. You should not grip or choke utensils. You should make a minimum amount of noise with your flatware.

- The pasta spoon - You may be given a spoon with your dinner of spaghetti or linguine, etc. This spoon is for twirling your noodle onto your fork. You should hold this spoon in your left hand and use your fork in your right as you normally would.

- Do not lick any of your utensils, especially your knife. The knife should at no time be near your mouth. If you wish to clean food from your knife, you should scrape the flat side of the knife across a tine of your fork, and repeat for the other side of your knife.

- Do not point or wave your utensils.

Close your menu when you are ready to order.

Table Manners Guidelines

Guidelines:
Ordering from a Menu

If there are items on the menu that you are unfamiliar with or unsure about, it is proper to ask your server questions pertaining to the item(s) in question. Appropriate questions to ask are: How is the chicken prepared? Would you recommend the New York Strip or Rib Eye? Inappropriate questions are: "This doesn't have mushrooms does it? Because I hate mushrooms" or "What in the world is a caper? I've never heard of capers."

You will fare better if you find out in advance that a dish is prepared with ingredients that you dislike or are allergic to, than to get your meal and pick around unwanted ingredients or even worse, experience an allergic reaction that would undoubtedly ruin your meal.

During a business meal, avoid ordering menu items that will be a distraction in managing or eating, such as pasta or ribs.

Guidelines – Breaking & Buttering Bread

Proper way to butter bread

Use your fingers to remove bread from the serving plate. When a bread and butter plate is on the table, use it appropriately.

Break slices of bread, rolls and muffins in half or in small pieces never larger than one bite. Butter each bite at a time. Small biscuits do not have to be broken. It is never appropriate to cut a roll with a knife.

When the rolls are served in a basket, take one, and always pass the basket to your right. Place the roll on the bread plate, which is located on the left side of your place setting. Never tear your roll in half or into many pieces.

Butter can be served on a butter dish with a butter knife; sliced in pieces on a small plate with a fork; or whipped on a small plate with a butter knife; or in a wrapper or a tub. You may use your own knife or fork (if clean) to retrieve butter from the serving dish and place it on your plate, if no utensil for that purpose is provided. However, if butter is served in a wrapper or tub, leave the butter packets and wrappers or tubs on your bread plate after you have opened and emptied them.

> **BUTTER DO'S & DON'TS**
>
> Butter each piece rather than the entire roll
> Butter the bread while it is on the plate.
> Never cut your roll.
> Never tear your roll in half or into many pieces.

Table Manners Guidelines

- Servers serve to the left and remove service items from the right.

- Dishes are passed counterclockwise (to the person to your right).

- Serving dishes and pitchers with handles should be passed with the handle toward the person receiving it.

- Pass salt and pepper together.

- If you want something that is being passed to someone at the far end of the table, it's okay to help yourself as it goes by as long as you don't take the last serving.

- Never serve yourself with your own silverware.

- If you're a guest at a dinner party, it's a good idea to wait until the hostess offers seconds.

- When passing your plate for seconds, leave the knife and fork on the plate and be sure that they are far enough on the plate such that they do not topple off.

- If there happens to be a bug, a piece of hair or other foreign object in your food, discard it inconspicuously. Notify the waiter quietly.

- Don't spit in your napkin. Unassumingly remove unwanted food (meat that you have chewed but can't swallow) from your mouth using the same utensil that it went in with. Place the piece of food on the edge of your plate. If possible, cover it with some other food (lettuce) from your plate.

- When food arrives, do not season it before you taste it.

- Don't encircle your plate with one arm while eating with the other

- Don't lean into food. Bring it up to your mouth.

- Never blow your food to cool it; wait for it to cool on its own, enough for you to eat it.

- Don't slurp soup, liquids, or pasta.

- Do not talk with food in your mouth.

- Chew with your lips closed.

- Wait until you have swallowed your food to take a drink.

- You may use a piece of bread to push food onto your fork if you need to or you may hold your knife in your left hand and use the knife to push the food onto the fork.

- Don't use tooth picks or pick your teeth with your fingers at the table.

- Keep conversation light. DO NOT discuss gory topics (i.e. details about a medical procedure, dental work, graphic accounts of accidents that have taken place, etc.).

- If you must be excused before others have finished, always say, "Excuse me, please."

- Don't push back your plate or stack dishes when finished. Wait until dishes are removed.

Guidelines – How to hold your own (Glass that is…)

| water | brandy | white wine | red wine | burgundy | champagne |

Glasses come is various shapes and sizes. A description of each glass shown above (from left to right) follows.

- **Water:** Water glasses have a full body and a short stem. Hold the glass by the stem to preserve the chilled temperature of the water.

- **Brandy:** Brandy snifters have a wide bowl and very short stem. Roll the snifter between both hands and then cup it in one hand – warming the glass brings out the bouquet in brandy. The brandy or sherry glass goes with the soup course.

- **White wine:** White wine glasses have a much longer stem and a much smaller bowl than the brandy glass; however, its bowl is sized adequately to capture the bouquet. It is slightly smaller in height than the Red, Burgundy and Pinot Noir glasses mentioned below. Hold the glass by the stem to preserve the chilled temperature of the wine. The white wine glass goes with the fish course.

- **Red wine (Bordeaux):** Red wine glasses are slightly taller than white wine glasses and also have a large bowl and a narrowed rim which concentrates aromas toward the nose. The bowl is slightly smaller than the Burgundy and Pinot Noirs glass. Hold the red wine glass at the bottom of the bowl where it meets the stem. The red wine glass goes with the main course.

- **Burgundy and Pinot Noirs:** Burgundy wine glasses have a broader bowl than a Bordeaux glass. The extra wide bowl brings out their complexities and allows the aroma to drift up toward your nose. Hold the glass at the bottom of the bowl where it meets the stem. Red wine glass goes with the main course.

- **Champagne:** Champagne glasses are tall and narrow fluted glasses adequately shaped to enhance the flavor of sparkling wine and keep the bubbles from dissipating. Hold the glass by the stem to preserve the chilled temperature of the champagne. Champagne will be served at the beginning of the dessert course.

Guidelines – How to Hold your Glass

Each glass will be filled appropriately with each course and then removed when the course is finished. If you do not desire to have wine, do not turn a wine glass upside down. Instead, allow the server to pour the wine. It is acceptable to hold your hand over the wine glass to signal that you don't want any wine.

Hold each glass like this…

- Hold wine glasses with clear colored beverages (water, white wine, and champagne or sparkling wine) by the stem to preserve the chilled temperature of the beverage.

- Hold the other glasses (brandy, sherry, burgundy, and red wine) at the bottom of the bowl where it meets the stem; warming these glasses brings out the flavor of the wine.

Hold your wine glass by the stem, not the rim.

Guidelines - Finger Food

Asparagus
Artichokes
Grapes
Hotdogs
Hamburgers
Pizza
Sandwiches
Tacos/tortillas

Certain foods are better suited to eating with your fingers. If you are ever in doubt, however, it is wise to use your fork. Most fast-foods are designed to be eaten with your fingers including pizza, french fries, hamburgers, sandwiches, and fried chicken. Use your fingers to eat olives and other hors d'oeuvres. Smaller fruits, especially those with stems like grapes and berries, are more easily eaten with your fingers. Certain vegetables are commonly eaten with fingers such as artichokes, asparagus, pickles, and corn on the cob. Bacon can be eaten with the fingers if it is crispy because it will most likely crumble if eaten with a knife and fork. Bacon can be eaten with a knife and fork if the bacon is limp.

Guidelines – Appetizers

Seafood
Save some for others
Don't eat all the shrimp

Chips & Dip
Don't double dip (dip a chip, bite a portion of the chip, then dip the chip again)
Don't overload your plate

Kabobs
Point the tip down and use the fork to take or slide meat/veggies/fruit onto your plate, one chunk at a time.

Caviar

To preserve the full flavor of caviar, scoop it out using mother-of-pearl utensils, wood or plastic. NEVER use metallic utensils because metal interferes with its intense but delicate flavor. Plastic utensils are never acceptable.

Caviar should be scooped from the container vertically from top to bottom to avoid crushing the eggs.

If caviar is passed to you in a bowl with its own spoon, serve a teaspoonful onto your plate. Caviar may be accompanied by toast points, high quality crackers, lemon slices, sour cream, minced onion, or deviled eggs. As the accompaniments are offered, use the individual serving spoon in each to take small amounts. Assemble a canapé to your taste with a knife; then use your fingers to lift it to your mouth.

A canapé (noun \'ka-nᵊ-pē, -ˌpā\) is an appetizer consisting of a piece of bread or toast or a cracker topped with a savory spread (as caviar or cheese). Canapés are held in the fingers and often eaten in one bite.

If you're at a cocktail party or reception, where prepared caviar canapés are being passed on trays, simply lift one off the plate and eat.

The Essentials of Dining Etiquette — 47

When you are being served caviar as an hors d'œuvre, no matter how much you might be tempted to over indulge, limit the number of servings to about two spoonfuls.

It's considered bad taste to eat more than about two ounces (about two spoonfuls).

Guidelines – Appetizers

Appetizer

If cheese is served as an appetizer, such as cubes on toothpicks, it is eaten with your fingers. If you are served a wedge of cheese, such as on a cheese plate, a slice of cheese is cut from a wedge, placed on a cracker, and brought to the mouth with your fingers.

Informal Meal

When sliced cheese is served as an accompaniment to a dish, such as apple pie, it is eaten with a fork.

Use a tooth pick or fork to pick up appetizers from a serving tray. Do not use your fingers.

Desserts

If served on little papers, pick up the dessert and the paper and place on your plate. Leave the paper on your plate until you have finished, and then discard the paper.

The Essentials of Dining Etiquette

Eating pasta – spear a few strands and gently wind the pasta onto the fork

Guidelines

HOW TO EAT DIFFICULT FOODS

Pasta

Flat pasta is always cut with a fork, not with a knife, and eaten with a fork. Spaghetti may be eaten with a fork and a spoon. When eating spaghetti or string pasta with a fork and a spoon, the spoon is used as an anchor: spear a few strands of pasta with the fork, then twirl the tines of the fork into the spoon so as to wind the pasta around the fork to take a bite. When eating string pasta, it is appropriate to use a fork. An easy way to master it: Spear just a few strands as you hold your fork at a slight angle to the plate; gently turn to wind the pasta onto the fork; and then bring the fork with the pasta to your mouth. Slurping pasta is never proper!

Lobster

Start by twisting off each of the lobster's claws at the point where they are attached to the body. Using a lobster cracker or nutcracker, crack open the claw and claw pieces.

Use a lobster pick to remove the meat from inside the jointed claw sections. Eat with a small lobster fork that has been provided.

When you've finished eating the lobster's claws, prepare to extract and eat the meat from the lobster tail. Use your fingers to detach the tail from the body by twisting the lobster tail until it separates from the body. Insert your thumb into the flipper end of the lobster tail and force the meat out with one push (you can use a sharp knife to slit the underside of the tail shell and use a small lobster fork to extract the meat). Use your knife and fork to cut the lobster tail into small bite size pieces and eat.

Gently twist each of the lobster's legs away from the body. To loosen the meat, bite down hard on each leg section. It is acceptable to suck the meat from the leg while indulging in this process.

Eating Soup - Scoop soup away from you.   At Rest – Soup spoon remains in bowl.

Soup

If the table has been preset, your soup spoon will be to the far right of your place setting. If there is no soup spoon you may use a teaspoon.

With your soup spoon in hand, scoop the soup away from you as shown in the diagram above (Eating Soup).

Lift a 2/3 full spoon of soup slightly level with the bowl and hold before bringing the spoon to your mouth.

Sip your soup quietly from the side of the spoon.

Do not blow your soup. Allow it to cool before eating it.

To get the last bit of soup from the bowl, tip the bowl away from you and spoon as described above.

Put oyster crackers in your bowl at your discretion, but eat larger crackers with your fingers (do not crumble into the soup).

To eat bread while eating your soup, rest the spoon in your bowl and pick up the bread and take a bite. Do not hold the bread in one hand and your soup spoon in the other.

Rest the spoon in your bowl between mouthfuls as shown in the diagram above (At Rest). When you have finished eating your soup, place the spoon on the under plate of the soup bowl, on the right hand side.

Manners Basics

- Be on time or 5–10 minutes early.

- Dress appropriately.

- Do not draw attention to yourself by noisy conspicuous behavior.

- Be considerate.

Five Ways to Be on Time Every Time…

1. Do not check your email or voicemail minutes before you plan to leave home.

2. Prepare the night before.

3. Set your clocks ahead a few minutes.

4. Set reminders.

5. Fill your gas tank when it reaches 1/4 tank.

Dress Appropriately
for a Dinner Party

1. Look at your invitation for instructions stating "White Tie" or "Formal" or "Cocktail Attire" which will provide some direction on your wardrobe choices.

2. Check with the host of the party a couple of days beforehand if you are in doubt as to the dress attire expected for the event.

3. Jeans and shorts are never acceptable when invited to someone's home for a dinner party, except for BBQs.

4. For events where "business attire" is suggested, men should wear a sports jacket and slacks and ladies should wear matching pant-suits or skirt suits.

5. For a dinner party where "cocktail attire" is suggested, men should wear a suit and ladies should wear a dress or suit (pants or skirt) that is dressier than business attire.

6. When "formal attire" is requested, tuxedo's for men and evening dresses with a light jacket or other arm covering is acceptable for ladies.

7. When "White Tie" is requested, men should wear tail suit, white tie and vest and ladies should wear a long ball gown.

8. For any and every event, make sure that your attire fits correctly and has been cleaned and pressed in advance. Make sure that everything fits a day or two before the event to leave time for adjustments if needed.

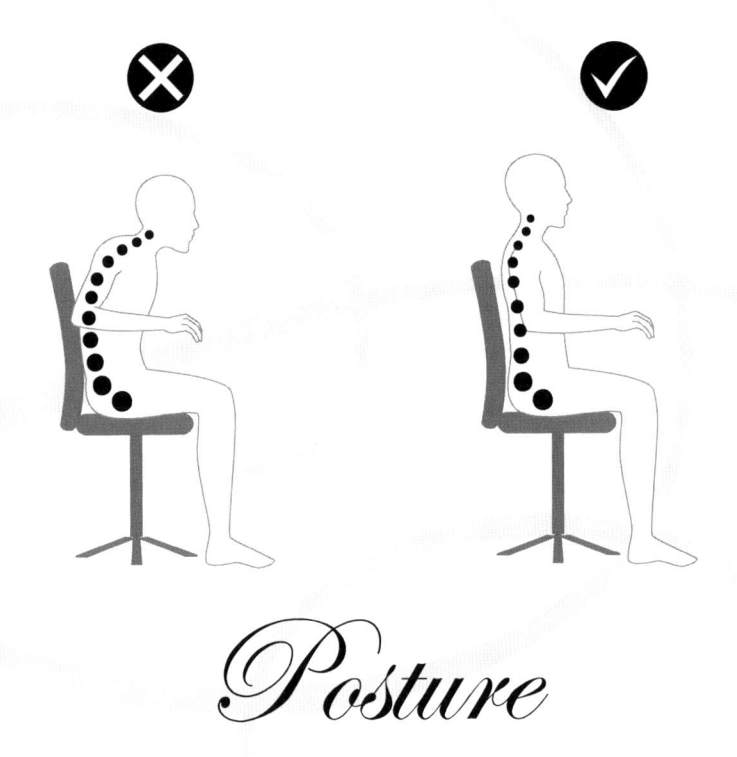

Posture

How Should I Sit?

- ஒ Sit straight with your back to the chair and both of your feet on the floor, not on the furniture.

- ஒ Do not lean forward.

- ஒ Do not sprawl your legs far enough under the table to encroach upon another's territory.

- ஒ Your elbows and forearms should be close to your sides (not on the table). Move your elbows forward and backward, not out to the side.

- ஒ Keep your hands in your lap (AMERICAN STYLE).

- ஒ Your wrists may rest on the table (CONTINENTAL STYLE).

Conversations at the Table

Engage in pleasant conversations (avoid controversial topics – sex, politics, religion)

- Imagine that the people at your table are on a small island – only the people at your table should hear the conversations at your table.

Sit high, feel high. Sit low, feel low.

Dinner Table Etiquette

Top 10 Do's

1. Be on time. If you realize that you will be late for a dining occasion, let the host or guest know as soon as possible. Lateness can be viewed as rude and disrespectful.

2. Dress appropriately for every occasion. Ensure that your clothes are clean, neat, and pressed.

3. Keep conversations at the table pleasant and light.

4. When you are ready to order at a restaurant, close your menu to signal to the wait-staff that you are ready.

5. Place your napkin on chair if you need to leave the table during the meal.

6. When food arrives, taste it before seasoning it.

7. Chew and swallow your food with your mouth closed.

8. When eating soup, rest the spoon in the bowl between mouthfuls.

9. Keep used utensils on your plate. Utensils should not touch the table after they have been used.

10. Take a sip of your beverage after you have swallowed your food. It is improper to take a drink from your glass with food in your mouth

Top 10 Dont's

1. Do not place cellular phones, keys, and other personal items on the table during the meal.

2. Do not groom at the table (i.e., fixing hair, applying makeup, flossing teeth, etc.).

3. If there is a buffet, do not begin to eat until 3 other people have joined you.

4. Do not point or wave utensils at anyone.

5. Do not make loud noises while dining.

6. Do not use utensils for anything other than their intended use. For example, do not use your knife to stir your coffee.

7. Do not hover or lean over your food, sit up straight and bring your food to your mouth.

8. Do not crumble larger crackers into your soup. Eat larger crackers with your fingers. Put oyster crackers in your soup bowl at your discretion.

9. Do not cut up meat all at once. Cut meat and eat one bite at a time.

10. Do not butter the entire roll. Butter and eat bread, one bite at a time.

DON'T PANIC

It's impossible for you to memorize every dining etiquette rule, but don't stress too much.

When in doubt, use common sense.

Notes

Notes

Notes

Notes

Printed in Great Britain
by Amazon